W

This book is due for return on or before the last date shown above: it may, subject to the book not being reserved by another reader, be renewed by personal application, post, or telephone, quoting this date and details of the book.

Carrying the Elephant
A Memoir of Love and Loss

MICHAEL ROSEN

PENGUIN BOOKS

PENGUIN BOOKS

Published by the Penguin Group
Penguin Books Ltd, 80 Strand, London WC2R 0RL, England
Penguin Putnam Inc., 375 Hudson Street, New York, New York 10014, USA
Penguin Books Australia Ltd, 250 Camberwell Road, Camberwell, Victoria 3124, Australia
Penguin Books Canada Ltd, 10 Alcorn Avenue, Toronto, Ontario, Canada M4V 3B2
Penguin Books India (P) Ltd, 11 Community Centre, Panchsheel Park, New Delhi – 110 017, India
Penguin Books (NZ) Ltd, Cnr Rosedale and Airborne Roads, Albany, Auckland, New Zealand
Penguin Books (South Africa) (Pty) Ltd, 24 Sturdee Avenue, Rosebank 2196, South Africa

Penguin Books Ltd, Registered Offices: 80 Strand, London WC2R 0RL, England

www.penguin.com

First published by Penguin Books 2002

1

Set in 10.5/14.75pt Monotype Minion
Typeset by Rowland Phototypesetting Limited, Bury St Edmunds, Suffolk
Printed in England by Clays Ltd, St Ives plc

dear e. love mx

Foreword

He wanted to make a mirror. Glass, mercury and a wooden frame – the perfect mirror. But he was no good at it. So he went to people he knew and asked them for a mirror. All they could give him were bits of old mirror. He took these home, stuck them on a board and hung it up. It's a mirror.

My father said the army reached Berlin
and he was billeted in an empty house. On the
shelves were the greatest works of German
Literature – Goethe, Schiller and the rest. And
Latin. Volume after volume. The house had
belonged to a classics teacher. Latin and Greek.
Very neat handwriting, my father said. He mimed
the handwriting with tiny movements of his thumb
and finger. On the sideboard there was the man's
photo album and at first he was a little kid, then
he was at school and then he was in Nazi uniform.
Stormtrooper or SS. My father didn't know which.
And the man wasn't there. He was gone. For years
I had no idea why my father told me.

Old gramophone horns and solitaire boards, you could see them through the window, and when we visited we got big fat raisins, I mean really big, really fat. His granny was Armenian and Uncle F lived with her. We knew he had boyfriends but we didn't know if granny knew. She gave us pilaff if our luck was in, though I left the almonds on the side of the plate.

Uncle F turned out to be the one who hated Stalin while my friend's dad, who was Uncle F's brother, was always in Czechoslovakia and the People's Republic. He brought back a set of pink Czechoslovakian plastic plates which were an example of how socialism was working and sang us a song about Barnacle Bill the Sailor. I'm coming, said Barnacle Bill. Or, I'm coming up, said Barnacle Bill, Barnacle Bill the sailor.
– A German worker goes to see Ulbricht, he said. 'Why haven't we got anything to eat, Comrade Ulbricht?' says the worker. 'Let me explain,' says Ulbricht. 'No,' says the worker, 'I don't want explanations, I want answers.' I heard that in Czechoslovakia off one of the German comrades, he said. You see, they can

laugh at the situation.

Then every so often he put on an old dinner jacket and went off with Uncle F and his boyfriends to see some Wagner.

It wasn't only that they said a naked woman cleans windows at the madhouse. They also said that they met up with Old Man Harris in the woods and they wanked him off into a bucket. I was in the High Street and H said, That's him. But I was to pretend to ignore him in case H got into trouble with his Mum. He said his Mum knew Old Man Harris but didn't know about the wank stuff.

They also said there was a secondary school kid called Colin who met up with them and they went to the path by the field and jumped on girls. One day in the summer we were asked into the Head's study, one by one and he said did I know about what had happened in the field by the woods? I said no and later back in class a kid called Rafter got called out and never came back.

It was a Formica table that my mother leaned on
when she said she never did understand why
Stalin got rid of his generals. He won himself
the breathing space to get ready and wasted it,
because of course Hitler would eventually go
East, we all knew that, she said. The people in
Leningrad were living off rats. You've never
seen starvation like it. Millions, millions dead.
You don't hear about it, but we knew. And you
waited for news. You always waited for the
news. And they go on about Alamein and Monty
but it was Stalingrad that turned it round, you
know. When we heard about that, it was the
first real good thing we had heard in years. If
we had lost at Stalingrad . . . it doesn't bear
thinking about. We wouldn't be here now.
One hand makes an arc across the table wiping
breadcrumbs into the hand waiting at the
table's edge.
Mind you, there were people here who wanted
Hitler to win. They'd've done a deal. We all
knew that.

We're bombing Egypt. Eeeeeeeowwwwwww! Stuart
is wheeling round the playground bombing Port
Said. At the weekend, I'm in Trafalgar Square, fingers in
the fountain water. Britain Out Of Suez. Britain Out
Of Suez. They're bombing Egypt. But we've got Nye
Bevan. He's come out against it. And he's here now.
It's a great turnout, they say. Bevan speaks. Then up steps
Martin's Uncle John. His lips are tight. 'They've gone
in,' he says, 'the tanks have gone in.' They all look
at each other, scared and tired. It's a blow. My father
puts his hand through his hair. My mother rubs something
invisible between her thumb and finger. It's that bad.
I'm thinking that Anthony Eden must have sent the
tanks towards the Suez Canal. 'They'll be in the streets
of Budapest by now,' John says.

It didn't seem odd to be eleven in East Germany in
1957. They were all teachers and my brother and I
played table tennis with them for hours. Or we played
it with each other while they went off to sit in rooms
and talk English. Hell, it was only twelve years after
it had all ended. We saw soldiers and rubble. There
was a day when they went off to Buchenwald and
came back frowning. My mother wouldn't say what
she'd seen, it was too awful to say, she said. Which I
wondered meant she was making it more awful than it
was. I don't suppose so. There was a row when one of
the Germans said he could remember the place where
the French delegate came from because he bombed it.
There was a row when John Holly and Len Goldman
disappeared. They were looking for women, people said,
and they mostly frowned about that too. But we got the
giggles, my brother walking up and down our room
doing the John Holly walk, the John Holly brothel-creepers,
head back, hands in the pockets, look at me, I can play
the guitar. Jesus, he must have been some teacher to have, I
thought. We couldn't breathe for laughing when we
looked out of our window and saw the horse with a willy
as big as an arm. My mother walked my father firmly
on when the women's group leader told us, as we stood

7

on the Unter Den Linden, that Hitler's favourite tree was
the Linden Tree. And I said, what's the matter with her
telling us that? Why shouldn't she? And there in Berlin
my brother took photos out of the coach window of a
giant slice of concrete tipped up, looming out of the
ground, just like chocolate cake. It's Hitler's Bunker,
he told me. A bomb landed on it. And there was a row
about Stalinallee. Did it or did it not look like a public
toilet? If it did, did that prove Communism had failed?
If it didn't, did that prove it was succeeding? I was
eleven, maybe it wasn't like that. But we kept doing
Goethe, Schiller, Bach and Luther: statues, houses,
castles, rooms, pictures, books and a bottle of ink
thrown at the devil. Twelve years to me now is no
more than an armsreach away. I can smell back that far –
no trouble. The things their heads must have been full of.
But we played on: 'You win, *dreizehn, einundzwanzig.*
Later I come and ask from you more English idioms.'

In the water they were very different, my father
keeping his head up, lying sidewise, stretching
one hand ahead, pulling with the other. Sidestroke,
he called it. It moved him through the water all right.
You could see that he didn't like being there, keeping
his mouth as high as he could, spitting. But my
mother rolled around in there. She could be lazy
with it, letting herself sink or rise, pleased that
her hair coiled and uncoiled over her face. Once
I looked down into the water and her eyes were
open in it.

There was someone called Max Ernst or Max Planck who came over on his bike with the Lit.

– Lit, Connie.

I could tell that my mother got tired of Lit. 'Soviet Literature', 'GDR Review', 'Germany Today'. Max would try to talk to her about Krushchev but she had exercise books to mark. In 'Soviet Literature' I read a story about a boy dying in Hiroshima who is nursed by an American doctor and with 'GDR Review' one month there was a booklet which showed pictures of Nazis who were judges and generals in West Germany. Globke. That was one of them. Globke. Max wore lederhosen.

My brother's girlfriends and near-girlfriends and if-only-they-were girlfriends were too much. They glowed in the dark. They smelled of lemon and cinnamon and rose; layers of it hung around our rooms for hours. They looked at us with sex-full eyes and disappeared off with him to his room, behind his locked door; of course it was locked, where I bet each one of them slipped out of her clothes and danced in front of him, driving him wild. I bloody bet they did, all of them, and they kept coming round and ringing on the door bell and standing in the doorway being ready. Until it went wrong and there was a bust up and I hated it and the girlfriend was gone and didn't come back. I hated that. But there'd be another one. Smelling so good.

I had just found and eaten a melon. In those
days you couldn't buy them in England. Orange on
the inside, marked out in segments on the outside. It
had been lying by the side of the road. In a pile. I
cut it into slices, shaved off the seeds, ran the
knife close to the skin, chopped the crescents of flesh
into chunks and fed them to myself off the tip of the knife.

Then I hitched a lift. The car was full of lavender. Three men
on the front seat kissing each other. They asked me if I went
to '*boîtes*'. *Boîtes de nuit*. Night boxes? Boxes of night?
The one with the sunglasses said, 'Night club.'
– No, I said, I don't go to night clubs.
Then they saw a Fiat ahead.
– *Un Italien*, *un Italien*, *un Italien*, they shouted.
They pulled the car alongside. On a two-way road.
One lane a side.
– *O Italien! Italien!*
120 on the clock, kilometres not miles.
Even so.
– *O Italien! Italien!*
He wasn't interested. They dropped me off at Montpelier.
– *J'espère que vous n'avez pas eu une mauvaise impression
de la France* is what I think he said.
– *Non, non*, I said, *pas du tout*.

H. M. Hyndman. The Origins of the Labour Party.
Essays have to be done. Hyndman? my father says.
You're doing Hyndman? Yes, I'm doing Hyndman.
A dark photo in a worn-out book. The SDF. The Social
Democratic Federation. Keir Hardie. The 1890s. All
that.
Oh, you couldn't mention Hyndman's name in front of
my Zeyde, he says.
His Zeyde. An old man in the 1930s. Maybe he knew
Hyndman.
Zeyde hated him from the time he supported the war.
He sold them out. Imagine: one moment all over Europe
they said they wouldn't fight and the next, millions of
them were dead. Thanks in part to Hyndman. What
else have you got? Stuff. What stuff? Chartism.
Chartism? What have you got to do on Chartism?
Why Chartism Failed. Failed? Failed? Chartism didn't
fail. What do they think they're doing telling you that?

Zeyde = grandfather

I came through the customs with my rucksack on
and the man asked me if I had anything to declare
and I said yes I had a big nail and a bottle of
brandy.
– What's the nail for? he said
– I collect them, I said.
– Yes, but what do you do with them?
– I put them on the mantelpiece, I said.
– Can I see the brandy? he said.
So I took out the bottle and he said,
– You can't take that through unless you pay
the duty on it. You're only allowed a half bottle.
That's a threequarter bottle.
– That's OK, I said, I'll pour away the extra.
So I opened the bottle there in the queue and got
ready to pour it on to the ground, and I said,
– You tell me when I've poured enough out?
– Sure, he said,
but the bloke behind me said,
– Hey, I could drink that. Don't pour it away.
– Is that OK? I said to the customs bloke.
– Yes, that's fine, he said.
So the bloke behind me got a cup out of his bag
and started pouring the brandy into his cup.

– Tell me when, I said to the customs man. You will tell me won't you?
– When, he said.

There was a typhoid outbreak in South America and they told us that we shouldn't eat corned beef. Don't eat corned beef. Don't eat Fray Bentos. My mother went to the cupboard and it was stacked up with corned beef cans. We always had cupboardsful of supplies. We must never be short of food. Ever. Families of friends might walk in. She took one of the cans down and looked at it. 'Better not open that till the typhoid outbreak dies down,' she said. This went into the family anthology: this is the way Connie thinks upside down. But when I re-run her taking the can down from the cupboard I catch sight of her looking sideways. She looks at us sideways before she says her line. And one of her eyebrows is up. And it was her, wasn't it, who used to say, 'Ask your father what he's doing and tell him to stop it.' When I was seventeen, I come home late after circuit training – chin-ups, bench-presses – and the house is dark. No one in. That means it'll be down to me to make myself a pile of honey and raisin doorsteps which I'll eat on my own listening to Big Bill Broonzy. But she's sitting there. Sitting in the sitting room with her elbows on the table, her hands under her chin, looking at a space just below the curtain rail. She hadn't bothered with the lights.

The first I knew about it I was in hospital but they told me I had been walking along in the road when I was hit. The bloke driving the car had driven on a couple of miles to the police station and told them he thought he had hit someone. So the cops came out and couldn't see anything. It was a stretch of road alongside a field. They figured he was sozzled and had imagined the whole thing so they were getting ready to go when they heard me. I was down a bank some way off, talking.

So it seems like I told them everything. Who I was, who my doctor was, where I'd been and they laid me out on the bed in the hospital. But it was night so the X-ray people had gone home and they didn't get there till 4 in the morning. Then I started peeing blood and that got them worried and the X-ray showed them my pelvis had come apart at the front. It wasn't broken. Just come apart.

They put me in a kind of sling and hung me from the bar over my bed, so my own weight pulled me together and that's where I found myself in the morning. It was all news to me. It happened, but I didn't know. I was lying in a ditch talking and I don't know a thing about it. I got the name of the doctor wrong. I told them the old one, not the new one.

It was in Leeds and he explained that there was no point in dressing in the morning. At night he'd go out on the piss, come back, shower, change into his work clothes, jeans, T-shirt, boots and into bed. When the alarm went in the morning, he'd kick the covers off, downstairs, and straight out the door.

Lenny let it be known that he and his wife were interested in finding out what all the fuss was about so would I be so kind as to come to dinner where they and other interested people would like to ask me some questions? The university is nothing to do with Vietnam, they said. Protest as much as you like but there's no need to do all that occupying stuff and Enoch Powell is entitled to speak for godssake. I think there was someone there who drew unbelievably badly for the *Daily Telegraph*. We don't see any connection between you complaining about how we teach and the Americans bombing North Vietnam. Protest as much as you like but do it peacefully and don't blame us. Then Lenny's wife said, Lenny, we left South Africa because we gave up on any peaceful way out, do you remember? Lenny, she said, we know that the only way Apartheid is going to end is through armed struggle. Lenny sighed but got into trouble because when he became Lord Hoffman he forgot to tell someone something important and General Pinochet was let off the hook.

In the 1940s English parents homed in on a
handful of names. Twenty years later I heard
my door being smashed. A guy rushed in and
jumped on me. He yelled, Mike, you bastard.
He looked at the person in bed with me and said,
Oh God, I'm sorry I thought you were Mike.
And he left.
But you are Mike, she said.
I know.
So who was that?
That was Mike, I said.

Dame Helen sat in her crimson tabard and
explained that I had completely and deliberately
misinterpreted the Question on Elizabethan
Comedy. She turned to the other eleven examiners
and explained that instead of considering the
Classic playwrights of the period, Mr Rosen
has written about a variety of obscure Burlesques
and Romances apparently put on by tradesmen
and the like. This was, she thought, a misplaced attempt
on Mr Rosen's part to show the context of Shakespeare's
mockery of the Rude Mechanicals presenting 'Pyramus
and Thisbe'. As a consequence, she would
discount this Question altogether from the Paper that
she marked, which, as the eleven examiners could see
from the sheet in front of them, gives Mr Rosen a gamma.
Mr Rosen, I see you haven't answered a question on
John Donne, surely the most important writer of the
Period, do you know what a paradox is? I said
I thought it would be a paradox if I got a First after
all this and she said, it wouldn't be a paradox, Mr
Rosen, it would be an irony or at best inappropriate.
It seems as if Dame Helen, troubled by the possibility
that I might have invented some completely bogus
Elizabethan comedies, had paid the Bodleian library a

secret visit, and ordered up from the stacks, the burlesques and romances I had written about. I did so like what you wrote about *The Canterbury Tales*, said one of the eleven gentlemen. Back at my flat I found out that Howard Marks had smashed my speakers.

Early days at Broadcasting House, I was in a corridor
when I heard the *Moonlight Sonata*. It tinkled out of
a door. Who's in there? That's Uncle David. They couldn't
bear to sack him when they closed down *Children's
Hour*. So they gave him a room and a grand piano and
he sits in there all day playing it. He was heartbroken
about *Children's Hour*. He's in the Drama Department
now. He came to a departmental meeting, and said that
he thought the document on Cost Benefit Analysis
was a terrible mistake. It was the sound of 'Hello, children,
everywhere.' That was him sitting right there. He fell asleep
during an argument between Bob the Texan Maoist
(a frequent visitor to the Chinese Embassy over
the road, 'Mike, have you been to Albania? It's socialism
in miniature') and Martin, the world expert on
absurdist theatre. The one they called Reggie,
played by Kenneth Branagh in *Fortunes of War*,
was asleep too.

First the GI runs round an assault course, then they give him LSD. He tries the course again. This time he flops about all over the place. By the time he gets back, his eyes are rolling. 'Soldier, you got a button loose.' 'Yeah, I got a button loose.' He keeps trying to fit the button through the hole. 'I got a button loose here. I got a button loose.' It was at Fort something. Sometime in the 1960s. We put this in the film and that's how it was shown. I heard we got a letter from the American Embassy. It said something about how they would like us to drop that bit. Something like that. There was a blond bloke in charge of me. I said, you don't have to take any notice of that sort of thing, do you? He cut it out for the repeat.

I don't think this matters much, but I was
standing by the phone, talking to one of those
tweedy ladies who used to run children's book
publishing and I was waiting for her to tell me
whether she liked my stuff or not. It would be
my first book and she was saying how she'd
taken the poems home and read them to her
son Harry and the thing is she had rung me first
thing in the morning. I had jumped out of bed
to get the call, so I wasn't wearing any clothes. I
was standing there with no clothes on waiting for
her to tell me if she wanted to publish these things
and I was dying for a pee. Dying. But I couldn't
say to her, I'm dying for a pee. Or I want to go and
do a pee. She was going to tell me if she wanted to
publish the poems or not. So I went on standing there
and she started to tell me how Harry did like them but.
And I thought, but? But? What but? But I didn't dare
and I was squeezing the end of my willy. And I
squeezed it so hard that it started bleeding. Right
by the hole. And then she told me that she wanted to
publish the poems and I was wild. I was that pleased
that I was crazy and she went on telling me that Harry
had really really liked the poems. There was a but, but I've

forgotten the exact but. And then in the end she rang off
and I dashed off for a pee and it was all red. And ever since
then when I pee, it goes in two directions. Two jets, one
straight out, and the other one has to deal with the scar. So
when I do a pee, I do it like a woman. I sit down.
Like I said, it doesn't matter much.

Who's in the room? My father, my brother, me.
Her doctor. She came home to die. She
didn't want to do it in that Victorian cubicle.
Not that I had that conversation with her. Like I
never had a conversation with her about the baby
that died before I was born.
So I had stepped back. I reckoned she needed other
people to deal with the things I didn't understand.
I nodded and smiled from a distance. Then one
morning there was some shouting. We rushed in.
She sat up and lost it. Now I see the other person,
the one who steps forward and catches what comes
out, scrumples up the cloth and vanishes it. Not
young. With glasses, no make-up. A face and
neck that crinkle. Big hard hands. And she's
Irish. So often in the room at our births. Probably
had a hand in the building of it, and here too.

I opened a Sunday newspaper and found out that
Brigadier Ronnie Stonham had been watching me.
It seems that he had lived in room 105 – not any more,
according to a spokesman. I had heard about
someone who had appeared one day at university
to check out if I was all right. But Brigadier Ronnie
Stonham was news to me. I had thought that I got
chucked out because I couldn't get up in the morning.
That damn thyroid gland. But according to the paper,
it seemed as if it was down to Brigadier Ronnie Stonham.
Roger from personnel had told me that the posts just
weren't there, Mike. Head of Staff Training had told
me that it had been great to have me on board but they
thought it would be better if I went freelance. I wrote
to someone the other day and asked to see the file that
Brigadier Ronnie Stonham compiled. I got a letter back
saying that we don't keep files. Not any more.

Pallister explained that the greatest threat to
Australia came from the North Vietnamese. There's
an alliance between these people and the Aborigines,
he said, and Australia will be destroyed if we don't
look out. There was a phone call and he moved
himself fast to get a syringe and pack a bag.
He left to inject someone causing problems. He
said I had to see the Bogong High Plains and while
it was over 40 degrees Celsius in Wodonga, me and
him went on our own to where it was cold and the
drovers used to walk their cattle. He wanted to
show me the oldest drovers' hut in Australia. We
found it, next to a dead tree. There were squares
of tin nailed to the walls to protect them from wind.
They were the flattened-out cans that carried their
food. He stroked them and said this is what he
wanted to show me.

I got a summons. It said I had been selling Chanel No 5 on the pavement in Oxford Street. I wrote back saying they'd got the wrong bloke. I haven't ever stood in Oxford Street selling Chanel No 5. They wrote to say I would have to be in court. I sent them a biog taken from a publicity file and I told them I could get a letter from someone saying that I don't sell Chanel No 5 on Oxford Street. They wrote to say I had to be in court. In court the lawyer for the council said I had been caught in Oxford Street selling Chanel No 5. I said I didn't need to sell Chanel No 5 in Oxford Street, I do other stuff. The magistrate said that it said on the charge that it was me that had been caught selling Chanel No 5 and hadn't I received the summons at my address; could I confirm that? Yes, I could confirm that. And that is your name? Yes, that is my name. So, she said, wasn't it reasonable to believe that it was me who had been selling Chanel No 5 on Oxford Street. I said, isn't it his job to prove that it was me selling Chanel No 5 in Oxford Street? She said, the man who claims to have apprehended you isn't here. You said that it wasn't you selling Chanel No 5 in Oxford Street, can you prove that? And I said that I wasn't sure that it was down to me to prove that I'm

me. Even if it was down to me, I wasn't sure that I
could prove that I was me. Not on my own.

We were on our way to San José or on the Santa Monica thing when Ringelblum said he thought things were looking good for me but he had messed up. All he had in his fridge were bowls of polenta and tiny boxes of Sun-Maid raisins. His daughter picked when she came to stay and we went to an old green pool to watch her train for the college swimming team. Then his son turned up too. There was some kind of trouble with his talking. It came out in lumps.

– I messed up, Ringelblum said, but I've got someone in Michigan. You though, you're doing good.

– Well, I said, maybe, but sometimes I wonder if I'm crazy trying to support seven people on what I do.

– That's the world's first McDonald's there, he said. You can buy jeans for 20 dollars at Crazy Joe's.

– You know what I like? I said. Going round the corner to Noah's, buying a cinnamon bagel, crossing the street, buying a magazine, and sitting right there and eating the bagel, and reading the magazine.

Ringelblum said – I could make it work for you out here. Does your wife like it here?

– She loves it. She bust her kishkes to come here in the 70s.

34

– I never heard that. Kishkes I heard. Bust your kishkes –
that I never heard.
I needed him to take me to a kids' bookstore to buy 'The Old
Woman Who Lived in a Vinegar Bottle' for her. It was a joke
between her and me about her always wanting more.
When I got back to England she wasn't there. Said she
got held up. It was lies. She was seeing someone else.
On the phone Ringelblum said he sounds like an asshole.
But she told me she likes assholes, I said. Told me six
months ago. I thought she meant me.

kishkes = guts

He did up the outside. Made a nice job
of it. Every window frame given a couple of
coats. All the brickwork pointed, the flashings
sorted, new gutters put in. The door and the
architrave were given three coats. New fittings.
The whole thing was perfect. Perfect. Inside
though, it was a mess. No other word for it.
Paper peeling off the walls, boards missing,
skirting coming loose, damp everywhere. You
could smell it the moment you went indoors.
It hit you. In one of the rooms, the ceiling
was down. There were carpets around the place
but they were finished, rotted right through.
There were a few sticks of furniture lying
around, nothing you could use. A rickety
table, some broken chairs. I tell you, you
didn't want to look at the bed. You couldn't
live in it. No way. There was an old Hotpoint
in the kitchen but you wouldn't want to risk it.
And the cooker was an inch deep. The units
were hanging off the walls. It was a mess. No
other word for it. A mess. And the thing is
you'd never know from the outside. That's
the thing.

I think it was called Riddle's Creek and don't call
them eucalyptus trees or eucalypts or gum trees. Just
say gums. Say the one thing you remember is the smell
of the gums. I looked at houses with verandahs. Some of
them were green or dark red, each one bolted together out
of corrugated iron. Some looked like old British Railways
buildings but edged with a hood propped up on pillars.
Green, dark red, yellow.

I imagined a poster like Dublin's Doors, fifty Riddle's Creek
houses. I'd collect them. A series. Each one different in its
curves or colours but the same for being tinny. I only had
two hours but I drove the van faster looking for another one
and another one. I was the Venice tourist late for his flight.
One more slice of the thing seen to take home and display.
And these pictures were coming out uninhabited. No people.
But I didn't care. I was the collector.

I left them in a pile on the mantlepiece in a room where
a family fell apart and in the packing of boxes all 72
pictures disappeared. I put them in the saucepan that
I threw out. Or they're lying under dolls in the attic. Or
she stole them. And not one of them with a
face on it.

Some friends came over and we started chucking
stuff out into the road. Chairs, books, plates. The kids'
old toys. Then we got on to the heavy stuff: sofas, tables,
the telly. Then pictures came off the walls, any cupboard
that wasn't actually fixed and everything in it. A real heavy
chest of drawers my dad had picked up from a depot
somewhere. Cooker, fridge, washing machine. The
computer. Then we got to work on the carpets, pulling
them up with claw hammers, rolling them up and
flinging them out with the rest. In the end the house
was stripped. So then I went back in and put
charges in the corners of the rooms, jammed them under
the boards. A couple in each room – they were all linked
up to one detonator that I had taken with me into the road.
I pushed it down and the house blew up.

224 chairs. A picture of 224 chairs. In order from
1820 to 1993. It's a history of sitting. 224 different
ways of sitting down. Over 173 years. You could
sit up, sit back, sit in, sit on, sit along. There's
a chair you could slump in, a chair where you hardly
had room to put yourself on, a chair where you had
to sit in amongst some big fingers. You wouldn't
know there could be so many different ways to sit.
I put it on my wall. People like the one where it
looks like you're sitting in someone's hand. Is that
what people want? To sit in someone's hand?

The last night together. He lay on the sofa where
he loved to lie. He was feeling groggy he said. Didn't
watch TV. Tired as usual, I thought. So hard to
wind down after evening work, I thought. Staying
up late, seeing his Melissa. Kipping during the
day on the sofa here with me. He got up once to
check his Pager. Melissa was buzzing him. He seemed
fed up, aching. Just like his sister had the night before.
Lying just where she had been lying. Temperature, aching.
– Hey, I said, a book of riddles has come through the post.
They wrote round a set of poets and asked each of us to
write a riddle. I wrote one. I read it to him.
– Do you get it?
– Yes, he said, your bum.
– That's it, I said.

Your bum.
Yes, those were his last words.

There were ways of figuring how big he got.
Like where his eyes came to, face to face.
The way his finger-tips edged beyond mine,
hand to hand. His wrists peering out of
the ends of his shirtsleeves. The way the guys
couldn't keep hold of his body bag as they
tried to slide it down the stairs.

It wasn't a good idea to leave him in the morgue. He came back to the house and people went in to see him. His hair was still growing. A short blond fuzz came out round his hairline. I put my hand on his chest and it rustled. Under his shirt they'd dressed him in a bin bag. They must have cut him about to find out what happened. I mucked about with his hair. His shoes were where he left them. His shoes are where he left them.

Next door neighbour Rob works late, talks football, enjoys parties, goes running, washes up. He didn't drop in or leave a note. I didn't see him for several days. Those first worst days. Then, in the alley between our houses I saw him. He saw me. We stood face to face.

– Rather you than me, he said.

We went on standing.

– And best of luck Saturday, he said.

I thought, but the funeral isn't on Saturday.

– And he said, Arsenal playing Spurs.

There's a way we make it the loneliest moment
of all. Even our eyes are supposed to look inwards.
Dr Dave, who'd known him since he was a funny
fat baby, said he'd've drifted off, losing it without
knowing it. In the days around then, someone left
bags full of nails in markets, in a pub, with explosive
packed in to shoot the nails out. It worked. Others
were seeing their sons taken off in bags too. What with
it being Brixton, Whitechapel and Soho it wasn't
hard to figure the scheme. Sure enough, it turned out
that the bomber's head was full of swastikas and he hung
out with people who do what they can for the white
race. A high-up in the Met said he was acting alone.

I called Wayne and Phyllis in Chicago. 30 years earlier, was it, their Rich had been hit on the freeway. Wayne said how people are good. They do good things. I remembered how a year before we had sat on their floor and read the Dear Rich Book – his letters. People are good, he said. They'll all be good to you. Except one.

I knew something wasn't right next door. Our side used to shake every time Wilma put her foot on the sewing-machine pedal which was about every ten seconds 14 hours a day. She was an outworker for C&As running up pleated blue skirts. He mended cars on the street. Fords.

The sewing stopped and Wilma lay on the front room floor listening to Music for Lovers. Did that for a couple of weeks then left with the baby leaving David with the three boys. He didn't understand it, he had done his best but what can you do? Then someone broke a hole in his back fence, came into the house, went to the wardrobe and went away with some photos of the family. David said he didn't understand why anyone would do that but what can you do? We broke up too. The baby died – I mean she got to be 18 years old and died. It was meningitis. We went to the funeral and then our baby died – meningitis – he was 18 too and they came to his funeral.

dear joe, your wild noisy huge brother
is dead. I couldn't do what my parents did:
bring two boys, four years apart through the maze.
I don't know if I'll find my way as well
as they did, seeing as they lost one
back near the beginning.

thank you for your card. I can't answer your
question: 'What can I say?' as I don't know what
to say either. You're right, it is a loss. It reminds
me that I lost him. He was there. Then he
wasn't. Though in between, he was blue and
stiff and landed with a thud when 999 told
me to pull him to the floor. Yes, it is unfair and
cruel. It also makes me tired with a
tiredness that hangs on like a dog. It's nice of
you to say you'll always remember him. You won't.

dear Bank re: E.S. Rosen's account, the a/c holder
doesn't hold anything.
dear Fenwicks re: your forthcoming clothes Sale,
thanks for the handout, there's nothing to clothe
dear National Blood Service, he was proud to have
given but he hasn't got any

I haven't seen you for a couple of years and we meet at a friend's funeral. I remember that you've had a child and that you've been ill. You see me and you cry, you're overwhelmed. You ask me how it's possible for me to carry on. I wonder if I look like someone who looks like it's possible to carry on.

One of us fell off the boat. Look in our faces, read our eyes as we come ashore. One of us fell off the boat. We're back. In our homes, you can see that there are times when we hate surviving. There are times when we think how easy to have been him. One wave and gone.

We're travellers on the road, always on the
road. Sometimes joined by strangers who
become friends who walk with us a while,
a day maybe, a year, maybe more. Then we
part. Maybe they've got another road to go
on, maybe it's us who turn off. Either way
we don't see them again. There's someone I
walked with for nearly thirty years. I was a
little thing, a tiny thing, when I joined her.
Then after thirty years she went. There's two
others. I've been with those two guys till now,
walking on. Here's one, been walking with me
since he was a little thing too, still walking.
Others, many others. One I joined when she
was just over one, walking along. Another, been
with us for 13. And here's one I met up with
when she was 7. We got through about 10 years
on the road together but about five years ago she
found it easier to be up ahead somewhere.
I catch sight of her sometimes, we wave,
even meet up for a while. There's one who
left altogether. He was with us for nearly
19 and oh he kept us laughing on the way,
his jokes, his faces, his noise, he took up
half the road, you know.

In Paris where we went to find out what we
thought about him not being with us any more I
bought a card. It's from an engraving by
Jean-Baptiste Oudry (1755–1759) 'Les deux
aventuriers et le talisman', an illustration of one
of La Fontaine's Fables. A man is carrying an
elephant – bending under the weight of it. He bends
at the knees as well, head down, face to the
ground. What's more, the man is trying to
walk. He's struggling to take a step forward up
a mountain. Above him is a rocky shoulder and
across from him is an even bigger crag, overlooking
him. But he hasn't fallen over and he's got that
elephant gripped round its front legs. He's carrying
the elephant. Jean-Baptiste Oudry has made
sure that he'll go on and on carrying it. At least as
long as I've got it on my noticeboard. He's carrying
the elephant.

Only us. That's all-of-us. All there is, is an us until there isn't an us. Maybe it'll be one-of-us that goes, or some-of-us, or in the end the all-of-us who were once here. So, all that we've got is either us, or not-us. Nothing in-between. Or out-there. It's an us-for-a-while, then a not-us. In our case there was one-kind-of-us, one kind of way of being us, and now, with one less of us, there's another-kind-of-us. When that hurts I'm better with the me, when it's in some kind of us, even if it roars with being a new-us.

Barbara whose husband died in a car smash told me I'd have dreams.
– They'll be beautiful dreams, she said.
None came for a year. Then they started coming. He visits. He stands in his grey check overshirt. He knows he's died. Once he said he was sorry that he didn't tell me it was septicaemia. I said I was sorry that I didn't know it was septicaemia. Sometimes he's at a distance in the way he was when I would drop him off in Drury Lane in time for the matinee. Sometimes he's been close on the sofa doing his crazy hugs or lifting me off the ground with all his massive indestructible might.

He lost his life
His life was lost
We lost his life
I'm losing his life

I swerve. There are humps and pot-holes. If I try
to drive straight over a hump, it scrapes the bottom
of the car. So it's best to turn to the left or right so
that I take the hump at an angle. Not face on. The
pot-holes are harder. They hide, looking like ripples
in the road-surface, but as I get near they yawn.
My wheel rolls straight in, hits the far side and the
whole car jolts. What's hard, is that the holes are often
on the down-side of the humps. So even as I dodge
the hump I land in the hole. Sometimes I spot
the hole on the other side of the hump and at the very
moment I've worked out how I'll avoid it, I find
myself going straight over the hump, dead centre,
and it's scraping the bottom off some vital out-of-sight
part of my engine.

My dead boy once made a clock. Instead of numbers, he put 12 letters that spelled: How Time Flies. It fell off the wall and broke into pieces.
– Hey, how time flies, he said.

Here are the pieces. I'll stick them back together some time.

don't tell me that I mourn too much
and I won't tell you that you mourn too much
don't tell me that I mourn too little
and I won't tell you that you mourn too little
don't tell me that I mourn in the wrong place
and I won't tell you that you mourn in the wrong place
don't tell me that I mourn at the wrong time
and I won't tell you that you mourn at the wrong time
don't tell me that I mourn in the wrong way
and I won't tell you that you mourn in the wrong way.

I may get it wrong, I will get it wrong, I have got it wrong
but don't tell me

A cat's skin can recover fast from a cut. After
a night-out scratching, they come in and heal
themselves up. In hours the skin closes. It
knits together and they're up for more scratching.
The snag is the claws. They're covered in bugs
that get left inside when the cut closes over.
I thought my cat's wound had healed but he had
sealed in dangerous stuff.

I got a letter home saying that RE is compulsory. So I sent a letter back saying it isn't. They sent me a letter back saying but it is. So I sent them a letter back saying I've got the government papers saying it isn't and you're breaking the law saying that it is. And they sent a letter back saying OK it isn't and we'll write a letter home to everyone telling them it isn't.

An egg in salt water
– The salt water is for tears, the egg is for
food, life and hope.
– The egg is in the salt water, he explains, because
nice things should happen or promise to happen even
in the time of tears. Our Sunday gatherings and remembrance
banquets are eggs, then. And so, and so, and so is this
oval belly that the midwife is listening to.

I wrote her a letter explaining that I was sorry
it hadn't worked out, that I had hoped it would
but I could see that it wasn't really possible
she didn't have to worry and I was sorry if I'd
been a bit too eager on New Year's Eve and I'd
meant everything I said in the emails but I didn't
want to go on as we were what with me thinking
it was becoming more than it was.
I didn't blame her for me thinking that. She had made
it quite clear we were friends and she liked me
being in her life but that's it and I wrote it and was
putting it in the envelope and just about to go to bed
it was late when the door bell rang and it was her and
she said that it was sorted, they were both relieved it
was over, it had got so as neither of them wanted to say
it, they still loved each other but they wanted to do
different things, it had taken the whole weekend talking
about it but it was sorted. It was what they both wanted.
So she stayed and now we've got a baby and it's bloody
amazing. Bloody amazing.

Is this the kind of mosquito that buries its proboscis in your skin and releases a stream of bacteria into your blood that multiply every few seconds and invade every cell of your body working their way into the nuclei where they feed but in so doing release an antigen that breaks down the cell walls of every cell in your body so you end up drowning yourself from the inside?

No. There is no mosquito that does that.

Bloody music. I hate the way it infiltrates.
Its nasty line in eavesdropping on what's
going on inside. Good spying, because it
knows exactly when it can make you open
the can, uncork the bottle, break the seal on
the jar – all the nooks where you had hidden
the raw unchewed material. It hoiks it out
and waves it about in front of your eyes. Look
and remember, it says. You thought you could
lock this away? Can blood hide from a cat?
Can petrol hide from a flame? No more shall
this be concealed. Listen to me, listen to me,
listen to me.

I was between King's Cross and Euston on the Victoria Line when a guy stood up and started shouting. He was distressed. He looked like me and said that we all had to get out. Get out of the carriage, he kept shouting, get out of the carriage, he was English, with an educated kind of voice, get out of the carriage, you heard what I said, I don't like you. That was what he said at each of us, I don't like you, get out of the carriage.

At first no one moved. There wasn't anywhere to go, the train was moving. We were in the tunnel.
Another guy put his hand on his shoulder and
said, ease up man but the guy who looked like me said, I don't like you either, get out, get out, get out the carriage. I want this place empty, he said I want it empty now, get out the carriage.

Then people started moving away from him and he was pleased. Ah, now I'm getting somewhere, he said. People listening to me. And he smiled. By then we got into Euston and some people called the guard and they took him away. He explained to the guard that people had started listening to him.

The drunk woman on the bike,
riding in the wind,
her red cheeks flaming,
her big eyes big,
her fat lips fat.
The drunk woman on the bike
swaying and swerving.
I know her name,
but today
she's the drunk woman on the bike.

The old city behind the city is coming down and I
am taken through the rubble up on to
the roofs, through the attics, knowing I
am the last to see it. It's all coming down, but it
doesn't have to. It could stay. It doesn't have to come
down, it doesn't have to be bulldozed, and I'm on
my own in the rooms, looking down at the ground,
and across the rubble to the row of houses on the
other side, looking through their windows to
the open sky and it doesn't have to be like this,
none of it has to come down, none of it, and I'm
the last person to know.

You can do it with lettuce. He waved bits of lettuce about in front of the light. Usually you do it with barn-doors. The lamps direct light on to the set but if you don't put barn-doors on the lamp, then it goes everywhere. So the barn-doors give the light an edge, one side of the edge it's bright, the other side, the light doesn't go. You can do it with lettuce, he was saying. Look, like this. You don't need the barn-doors. He had big bits of lettuce, not iceberg lettuce, big leaves of lettuce, kept firm by the stalk running up the middle. See? It works. Lettuce does the job just as well. And he was right, the lettuce was doing well. But I was sure that lettuce was slang for something. I'm sure it's slang for something

I packed my books into fruit boxes. Boxes for
peaches, grapefruit and avocados. In the morning
all my books had turned into fruit. The two
volumes of the *Shorter Oxford Dictionary* were
plump pears. A book I've had since school. *The
Pageant of Modern Poetry* had become a banana.
Squeezed up against each other, books I've
looked after for years, travelling with me
from flat to flat, house to house, rolling around,
bumping up against each other, or snuggling
up to the cardboard walls of the boxes.

In days they would blacken and rot, unless
I chose to eat them. Sit there for hours
munching my library till I was fat and sick.

It turned out that the baby was in hospital.
Alone. No one else was there. She was sitting
up in a bed on her own when we got there. There
was a tube coming out of her nose but it wasn't
connected to anything. And she was sweating.
Her back was wet. Soon after, the nurses and
doctors arrived so I said this doesn't look good.

And they said you're right. Someone mentioned
fan fever, the fever you get from sitting too long
next to an electric fan. So then they got to work
connecting the tube and doing artificial respiration.
It was tense. Could have gone either way. But
she pulled through.

Later I was coming away from the place
and she fitted into the palm of my hand.
The size of a teacup. There was a bad moment
as I sat on the bus with her in my hand there.
She went still and cold. But I blew on her and she
woke up, stirred and looked around,
eyes wide open.

How shall we defeat The Enemy?
We shall defeat The Enemy by making alliances.
Who shall we make alliances with?
With people in whose interests it is, to be
   enemies with The Enemy.
How shall we win an alliance with these people?
We shall win an alliance with these
   people by giving them money and arms.
And after that?
They will help us defeat The Enemy.
Has The Enemy got money and arms?
Yes.
How did The Enemy get money and arms?
He was once someone in whose
   interests it was, to be enemies with our enemy.
Which enemy was this?
Someone in whose interest it had once
   been, to be enemies with an enemy.

The news was that the same cells that
had been digesting bacteria were
now digesting me. I was being consumed
from inside. The cells that were so good at
identifying alien organisms – ones that
had arrived through the usual holes:
mouth, nose, cuts and the like – had now
identified part of me as alien too. Did this
mean that they had tolerated me for twenty
years and then suddenly found me undesirable
and dangerous? Was it something I did? Or
was it the cells that changed? Previously
content, doing what they did best, but then
came under some influence which altered
their attitude and so started to eat me?

Now it seems they've stopped. It was only
one bit of me they were after. I had expected
that they would go on finding areas to consume
but they've left off. Part of me has gone but the
rest is still there. It seems as if it is possible
for them to start up again, finding new bits to
ingest and eliminate. I'll say that differently: it
seems as if it's possible for me to start up again,

finding new bits of me to ingest and eliminate. Once, when we were camping, and stuck in the tent for too long, we wondered if it was true that someone had survived by chopping off his hand and eating it.

My teeth are moving round my jaw. On the bottom rack there's one that's come out from the right and one that's come out from the left. Between the two gaps are ten teeth. And now they're shunting round. Like curtains round a bay window. Each tooth, wedged in tight to the next has started to nudge to the right. They're all leaning rightwards and this shifts them round in the groove in my jaw. Like when we stood at football matches, shoulder to shoulder, belly to back. Someone began a shove and it would move through the crowd.

Isn't their real name manila folders? but it says
they're Document Wallets. For years I've
filled them with the kids' first scribbles, letters
I didn't know how to answer, school photos,
newspaper articles that seemed too meaty
to throw. I label them with marker pens:
To Do; Car; Unwanteds. Now two red plastic
stacking boxes are full of sent-in stuff: bank
statements, invites, credit card offers. So I've bought
a pack of Document Wallets. They're 'files', aren't
they? Files for filing cabinets. No matter. Everyone
of them is unlabelled. I don't know yet which one
will be what. Like stem cells before becoming
legs or eyes. Could be either. Or a kidney. Which
bit of me is the blue one going to be? Or the yellow
one. I push some paper into the purple one and
write on it Bad Guides.

I was just crossing the road at the lights
when a girl said, You know my dad. Malcolm.
And you met his old girlfriend Geeta on the
Tube.
I was walking to the Bank but down the road
thirty years earlier hadn't their cooker burnt
them out of a flat, a terror to her, scalded and
scarred from a childhood accident? Wasn't it
her, with her angry eyes and white boots who had
whipped meetings with news from the third world?
Those long quivering vowels, a marriage between
Cheltenham Ladies College and Pandit Nehru. Malc
had done his bit of whipping too, jeering out of the
side of his mouth, at LSE bosses and US generals.
And didn't the three of us hit the Natraj in Whitfield
Street at 7, break the neck of American Imperialism
over roghan josh, tarka dal, brinjal bhaji, puri, raita,
and pistachio kulfi by 10 and be home by 11? But he
wouldn't live in Delhi. It broke them. He became a
sleuth, unpicking the secret accounts of company
directors, a kind of spying, I think. It seemed to
have started out as the unmasking of capitalist
intrigue. Turned into the info that one corporation
wants in its efforts to outwit another. Something

like that. He makes a living. And yes, I did meet
her on the tube. She was sitting opposite, in a
coat and sari. I recognized her when she looked
up from some papers. She's a lawyer in Delhi.
She makes a living.

We went to the Public Record Office to find out
what the Foreign Office had made of gangs of German
boys who didn't like the Hitler Youth. We had heard
that they used to go off to the park with girls, some
tied condoms to the back of a Hitler Youth Leader's
bike, one group burnt down a kiosk run by an SS man,
some passed food to French slave workers, some tried
to blow up a bridge, some got sent to a Jugendschutzlager,
some to Sachsenhausen or Ravensbrück, some were
hanged in public in the square in Cologne. While we
waited for the files to come, I looked through the index.
And the index of the index. I clicked on Foreign and
Colonial Office. I typed in Students and clicked
on Search. I refined the Search to 1967, 1968, 1969.
It said the status was Open Access, they were available
under the 30 year rule. I scrolled down the page: there
was Student Unrest, Student Riots, Student Disorder,
Foreign Students. Maybe twenty or more files. I could
order them up. Maybe our gang would be there. But the
files we were waiting for, arrived. We had to get on.
We were pushed for time. Like us, the FO chaps had
read the typed reports from an un-named source in
Germany and noted in handwriting on the top sheet
that these gangs didn't seem to be a very promising

starting point for the re-building of Germany after the War. It was suggested that once the occupation was established, the Army should set up Youth Groups and Boys' Clubs. One Major suggested a League of Chivalry. This should appeal to the Germans' love of regimentation and romanticism, he said, but it is rather a pity that the Germans don't know about our King Arthur and the Round Table.

On the way there on the Victoria Line there was just one of them. I'd say about 14, short with it, and an old man's pot belly. He had some kind of accordion hanging from his shoulder. A small red piano accordion. On the way back, there were three of them and now I could see that he was in charge. He sat opposite me shunting coins from his tracksuit top to his tracksuit bottoms. His two boys came through the carriage with another red piano accordion. Exactly the same. These two looked about 9. They had polystyrene cups for the money, most of us reading papers. It was midday, a weekday, a Thursday, in November, between Pimlico and Victoria. They were trying out a daisy cutter in Kabul.

This is the sick tunnel. People with tickets for the Tube are sick on the floor. Then they catch the train. But it's not there. The lumps and flob have gone. Sick-cleaners scoop it up and disappear it. The stink stays. It's always sick in here. A dog's nose could do things with this. It could write a Who's Who from the whiffs. He ate mushrooms. She drank tea. There's evidence from this one, the smell might reveal, of abandon, a wild night beyond the reach of office hours; evidence from another of despair, something about the days being relentless and overpowering. Sometimes it takes two or three retches to get it all out.

Pinter lost his patience. Perhaps he was right, what with Kent and me being so polite with the petition, expressing this, conveying that, letting our feet rest on the Embassy carpet. Until then, their men had let their eyes wander over us. In a lazy way, with a smile or a shuffle of the hand, they let us know we were duff, they were subtle. Their job was to preserve a beautiful balance: letting the enemy know that it could be obliterated, but keeping this out-of-sight from friends. They weren't going to upset the design by letting their prisoner go. Not that anything was said. Pinter, I think, sensed it. He's good on silences, isn't he?

– Don't think we're going to forget this, you know, he shouted. They didn't blink. Neither did the Berlin Wall, I was thinking.

It didn't work out the way it's supposed to. The four of us on a platform. We were supposed to have given up. We should have learnt that being unconvinced is what counts for wise. But we're here. Shocked again. Coming out of our kitchens to say, if nothing else, everyone here is sick of the age-old cruelties. We should have noticed that history ended but we got distracted by some massacres. So we're here again. It didn't work out the way it's supposed to.